Marriage

Is
So Much
More
Than A
Ring

Your Home
Should Be Peaceful

Dr. Carlisa M. Smith

ISBN: 978-1679158766

Contents

Acknowledgments

"My God, I give you all the honor and glory."First, I want to thank God for the many miracles and blessings He has bestowed upon me throughout my life. I thank God for good health and strength, and hearing my prayers. I would also like to thank my parents, Lucius and Gloria, for giving me life. I would like to thank my godmother, Barbara, for all of her encouragement, support, and believing in me. I want to thank my children, Jeffrey and Jelissa, for their unconditional love, support, and always believing in me and my dreams. I would like to thank all my immediate and extended family members and friends for their continuous encouragement and support.

He Proposed!

He put a ring on it!

The Big Day!

The Big Day!

The Big Day!

Mr. & Mrs. Moore

A Word From Dr. Carlisa

I've been in the real estate industry for over 26 years. During that time, I have met and spent time with married couples and people who were dating. I have even met single people who wanted to be married so badly that they were planning the wedding and had everything ready, the only thing that was missing was the groom.

Ironically, as many beautiful marriages as I have seen, there were many more that were horrible. I remember growing up in church and hearing that it was better to marry than to burn. No one wants to go to hell, so marriage was the "right thing to do." So we thought. Unfortunately, people were getting married without really knowing who they were marrying. This caused misery, stress, anxiety, and dysfunction for a lot of people; consequently, resulting in a very unhappy home.

God has given us guidelines for our protection so that we can have a happy life. As entrepreneurs and corporate decision-makers, when you are adding to your team you interview potential candidates before offering them the position. Have you done the same and interviewed your potential spouse? Before you fall in love with someone, think with your head and not your heart. Ask the person some questions to see if they are the person you have been trusting God for. Guard your heart.

Keep thy heart with all diligence;
for out of it are the issues of life.
Proverbs 4:23

When you choose a spouse, use wisdom, and select someone with the character and morals that you agree with. Additionally, select someone you are willing to commit to spending your life with, someone you want to be close friends with, have children with, and share everything with. Don't fall in love and give your heart to a stranger. The consequences may be too great. Looking good and being fine isn't enough for a lifetime commitment.

Marriage's Intended Foundation

We all may have our own interpretations of what marriage is or should be. Life's experiences, media, society, culture, people from church, the scriptures, your belief in God, or your faith may be the key influencers.

A commonly accepted definition of marriage is a religious union and ceremony that formalizes the decision of a husband and wife to unite their lives legally, economically, emotionally, and to live as a married couple. Furthermore, marriage is a relationship in which the husband and wife pledge themselves to each other and live their life according to the word of God. Marriage is for two complete people who are willing to give 100/100, not 50/50.

According to scripture,

Whoso findeth a wife findeth a good thing, and obtaineth favour of the LORD.

Proverbs 18:22

God has instituted order and structure in the home. We have to understand our authority in God's kingdom according to 1 Corinthians 11:3. The head of every man is Christ: and the head of the woman is the man: and the head of Christ is God. The levels of authority in the home, as given by God, are:

- ➢ God the Father
- ➢ Jesus
- ➢ The husband
- ➢ The wife
- ➢ The children

What is the role of the Husband?

The husband has the responsibility to lead by example. God says that husbands must be considerate and treat their wives with respect.

> *Likewise, ye husbands, dwell with them according to knowledge, giving honour unto the wife, as unto the weaker vessel, and as being heirs together of the grace of life; that your prayers be not hindered.*
> ### *1 Peter 3:7*

Don't take the word "weaker' partner to heart. In this scripture, God is referring to strength. Many women are stronger in character, stronger in faith, and stronger in determination than their husbands, which proves that God is, in fact, referring to the husband's physical strength.

Jesus said that husbands must love their wives as Christ loved the church. God commands the husband to give himself for his wife. The husband must make sacrifices if he needs to, in order to make sure his wife and children are taken care of. Husbands must provide for the family otherwise; the Bible says you are worse than a nonbeliever.

What is the role of the Wife?

The Bible says that a wife must submit to her husband's authority.

> *Likewise, ye wives, be in subjection*
> *to your own husbands; that, if any*
> *obey not the word, they also may*
> *without the word be won by the*
> *conversation of the wives;*
> ### 1 Peter 3:1

Most women are eager to get a ring and to be married so they will say "yes, I will submit to my husband"; but the test comes when the husband asks the wife to do something (or to not do something) that she does not agree with. When a wife doesn't submit, she is rebelling against authority, not the husband's authority, but God's.

A wife may ask if she has to obey her husband if he's not living for God, if he's not doing what he's supposed to be doing, and or if she has no respect for him; the answer is yes. If your husband asks you to do something illegal, you are not obligated to break the law. A wife is only obligated to obey her husband if it does not violate the word of God.

What if the wife is an ungodly woman? Proverbs 7 talks about how an ungodly woman behaves. The ungodly woman is loud and defiant. She defies anyone who tries to help her or give her advice and direction, and openly speaks aloud to them, rejecting their advice. Today's television shows and movies display the attributes of an ungodly woman and unfortunately, this behavior is copied by a large number of women. This makes it challenging for a husband that's living for God.

For at the window of my house I looked through my casement,
And beheld among the simple ones,
I discerned among the youths, a young man void of understanding,
Passing through the street near her corner; and he went the way to her house,
In the twilight, in the evening, in the black and dark night:
And, behold, there met him a woman with the attire of an harlot, and subtil of heart.
(She is loud and stubborn; her feet abide not in her house:

Now is she without, now in the streets, and lieth in wait at every corner.)

So she caught him, and kissed him, and with an impudent face said unto him,

I have peace offerings with me; this day have I payed my vows.

Therefore came I forth to meet thee, diligently to seek thy face, and I

Come, let us take our fill of love until the morning: let us solace ourselves with loves.

For the goodman is not at home, he is gone a long journey:

With her much fair speech she caused him to yield, with the flattering of her lips she forced him.

He goeth after her straightway, as
an ox goeth to the slaughter, or as a
fool to the correction of the stocks;
Till a dart strike through his liver;
as a bird hasteth to the snare, and
knoweth not that it is for his life.
Hearken unto me now therefore, O
ye children, and attend to the words
of my mouth.
Let not thine heart decline to her
ways, go not astray in her paths.
For she hath cast down many
wounded: yea, many strong men
have been slain by her.
Her house is the way to hell, going
down to the chambers of death.
Proverbs 7: 6-15, 18-19, 21-27

When considering marriage there are many areas to examine. It is better to take the time to learn as much about the person that you are considering committing to before you make the commitment. You don't want to look back when the relationship is over and say that you learned more about them at the end of the relationship than you did at the beginning.

Spirituality

Wherefore they are no more twain,
but one flesh. What therefore God
hath joined together, let not man put
asunder.
Matthew 19:6

Did you talk to God about this
relationship? Did God have anything to do
with this relationship or is this all you?
You don't want to find yourself lying on
the floor in a puddle of your own tears
asking God to forgive you for taking
matters into your own hands. You also
don't want to be unequally yoked.

Be ye not unequally yoked together
with unbelievers: for what
fellowship hath righteousness with
unrighteousness? and what

communion hath light with

darkness?

2 Corinthians 6:14

You should be seeking Godly character when considering a spouse. Godly character is simply doing things God's way. To have Godly character is to have the nature of Jesus; love, joy, peace, kindness, goodness, faithfulness, and self-control.

Believers usually desire to have Godly character. To develop this character requires reading the word, doing the word, and speaking the word. When believers read the word, they get the strength to obey the word. Having Godly character will help with daily decisions and will help with the connection and bond in a marriage. As you expose your heart to the Word, you will gain the inner strength to live right and honor your vows to your spouse.

When following the desires of your sinful nature, the results are very clear; sexual immorality, immorality, impurity, lustful pleasures, hostility, jealousy, outburst of anger, selfish ambition, division, and possibly a challenging marriage. If you are out of harmony with God, you cannot be in harmony with your spouse.

A double minded man is unstable in
all his ways.
James 1:8

You must truly love yourself before you can honestly give someone else your love. If your partner shows you signs that he/she doesn't love or respect you before you are married, you won't be able to change him or her after you're married. You want someone who can love you, but some people don't know how to love because of their life's experiences and personal beliefs.

Charity suffereth long, and is kind; charity envieth not; charity vaunteth not itself, is not puffed up, Doth not behave itself unseemly, seeketh not her own, is not easily provoked, thinketh no evil; Rejoiceth not in iniquity, but rejoiceth in the truth; Beareth all things, believeth all things, hopeth all things, endureth all things.

*Charity never faileth: but whether
there be prophecies, they shall fail;
whether there be tongues, they shall
cease; whether there be knowledge,
it shall vanish away.*

1 Corinthians 13:4-8

*The fear of the LORD is the
beginning of knowledge: but fools
despise wisdom and instruction.*

Proverbs 1:7

When your spouse or potential spouse is
too busy or acts as though they don't need
God in their life; this is a red flag.
Someone can have all the education,
money and/or fame and believe that they
are smart and wise. However, if they won't
commit to God, they're not going to fully
commit to you.

Some may believe that they know it all, have it all and don't need God. This is a true sign of a fool. Run!

Does this sound familiar - when you bring up God, your partner will argue and fight for "their rights?" They will argue about what the Word says, and you can't get a word in because they think they know better? Pride proceeds a fall.

Keep in mind that Proverbs 1:7 says that fools despise wisdom and instruction. If you see signs of lying, dishonesty and a long list of past relationships; don't ignore the signs. This is your intuition and the spirit of discernment. The common denominator in all the past relationships is them. If a partner cheats on someone else with you, they'll cheat on you too and may not fully commit to you either.

Communication

Can you communicate with others verbally, nonverbally, and in writing openly and maturely? Are you a good listener? Open communication is the key to understanding what the other person is saying. Communication isn't just hearing what was said but comprehending what was said.

Communication is crucial in relationships and marriage. The word communication is defined as imparting or exchanging information by message or otherwise. God gave us two ears and one mouth for a reason. Perhaps we should listen twice as much as we speak. It's ok to ask questions but listen to understand.

Nonverbal communication is a powerful connector. Are you able to display affection in public? It's ok to be physical, to touch when you sit on the couch, pass each other in the kitchen, touch in the car, hold hands, and to do the things you did when you first started dating. Touching is a powerful thing; it shows affection, offers intimacy, and communicates "I love you" without saying a word.

Statistics show that on average women speak 29,000 words a day and the average man speaks 12,000 words a day. When a woman with a gentle, quiet spirit speaks, it's encouraging and pleasant, like a sweet fragrance.

On the other hand, a woman who is full of bitterness, resentment, and jealousy could speak only ten words a day, and those ten words could be the words you wish you had never heard. The quality of words is more important than the number of words that are spoken. Most men would agree that a gentle and quiet spirit is more beautiful than the outward appearance of a woman.

A soft answer turneth away wrath: but
grievous words stir up anger.
The tongue of the wise useth
knowledge aright: but the mouth of
fools poureth out foolishness.
Proverb 15:1-2

Communication is extremely important in a relationship. If you want to know something, ask. Don't allow days to pass with your mind running wild. This leads to stress and creates doubt. Some of what you may perceive as small things should be discussed when you are getting to know your partner.

For example, what did dinner consist of when you were growing up? Let's say your partner grew up with his mother preparing a three-course meal every day and at dinner time the entire family sat down for dinner together. What if you came from a large family and you were accustomed to your mother making large pots of food, like spaghetti, to feed all of you and everyone would grab a plate and eat in different parts of the house or in front of the TV. If you don't know what your partner expects for dinner, based on what was experienced while growing up; it could cause conflict because of a breakdown in communication. Picture yourself preparing a big pot of spaghetti for your new husband, putting the plate in front of him, and he looks at you like you are crazy while you are dumfounded and devastated because he did not appreciate what you had cooked for him. A discussion about childhood experiences would have provided clarity. These are the types of conversations that should be had prior to getting married and can help you to determine if you should say, "I do."

Once you get married, continuous communication is vital. Being able to talk to your partner about anything before and during marriage is ideal. Some people indulge in watching excessive reality TV which causes their expectations to be distorted. This also contributes to some people needing drama in their lives to feel excitement.

With consistent communication, it's easy to talk about what's wrong without making it much bigger than it is and blowing things out of proportion. Stop, take a deep breath, and in some situations walk away for a while to calm down. When you revisit the conversation remember that communication involves listening as well as verbalizing your thoughts. Focus on a positive solution that will work for the both of you. Sometimes you may need to agree to disagree and leave it alone for the moment.

Trust

Do you feel safe? Are you willing to share your money? Would you feel comfortable sharing the passwords to your cell phone, computers, email accounts, your private secrets, and anything else you have near and dear to your heart? These are questions you need to consider when you want to get married. Marriage is one of the biggest investments you will make because you are investing your life with another person. Your spouse will be your life partner and should be there for you through everything. To have this type of relationship, respect and trust are required.

Respect is about trusting your life partner and treating each other the way you want to be treated. It is also about considering each other's thoughts before making decisions, talking things out, and working as a team. It is not a competition.

Finances are one of the major reasons that relationships don't work, trust in this area is vital. You both need to decide who will pay the bills. You will need to decide on an amount that you won't spend before talking to your spouse. Don't go out and buy big-ticket items like a car or property behind your spouse's back. You need to be able to trust each other in this area. I can't stress that enough.

I was taught that when you get married you put your money together. I tried that and it did not work for us. You must do what is best for your family. If you are married to someone and they are not good with money, one of you has to step up to the plate to keep you from becoming homeless. For example, if you are married to someone that's swiping the debit card (like they put a million dollars in the account) without saying anything, when you sit down to balance your account you may be in shock to see that the money is gone.

There are a lot of responsibilities that come along with the words, "I do." That is why trust is so important. You should be able to trust that your partner will uphold the vows they made to you.

When you are married to someone that honors their vows, it's beautiful. One of the best parts of being married is having a partner for life. After you have committed to each other, shared your vows, and exchanged rings, you have a best friend and life partner who is exclusively yours.

There will be seasons in your life and in your marriage where one of you will need to take the lead and be strong for the other. You should be able to trust that the other will do the same when needed.

Always speak positive things over your relationship. Whatever you plant in your heart will grow. You plant seeds in your heart by your words. Whatever you say with your mouth will go into your heart, and your heart will produce a harvest. If you speak doubt, unbelief, or failure over any area of your life, you will have that.

When you experience adversities in a relationship, you don't have to react or retaliate in the natural realm, respond with the Word, and fight the evil spirits that are influencing the situation.

For we wrestle not against flesh and blood, but against principalities, against powers, against the rulers of the darkness of this world, against spiritual wickedness in high places.

Ephesians 6:12

Sex

There is a difference between sex, intimacy, and love. Sex is a physical act and intimacy is emotional. Intimacy usually occurs outside of the bedroom.

What are your thoughts about sex? Was sex discussed in your home when you were growing up? Did you see your parents display love? Did your parents ever tell you that they loved you?

Your perception of love, sex, and intimacy can affect your marriage. Understanding your partner's love language will contribute to the wonderful and satisfying sexual experiences with your partner.

When you met your partner, you accepted each other the way you were.

You may have crazy personalities, usual laughs; you may have liked certain music or movies. You can talk about all the things you loved about each other when you first started dating. You need to remember those things because, as time passes in a relationship, people are inclined to try to change their partner.

Life will shape you. Allow your partner to be the person you married and never stop falling in love with who they are becoming. This will help to cultivate ongoing intimacy. It is imperative that the husband and wife make it their priority to fulfill each other's needs.

Let the husband render unto the
wife due benevolence: and likewise
also the wife unto the husband.
1 Corinthians 7:3

The wife hath not power of her own
body, but the husband: and likewise
also the husband hath not power of
his own body, but the wife.
Defraud ye not one the other,
except it be with consent for a time,
that ye may give yourselves to
fasting and prayer; and come
together again, that Satan tempt you
not for your incontinency.
1 Corinthians 7:4-5

As people get older, the sexual relationship may change. There are a number of factors that redefine the sexual experiences; such as illness, stress, and erectile dysfunction to name a few. Can you love your spouse during this? What if they could not perform at all and you become companions only? You must be able to love each other through it all.

Finances

As I have communicated with couples about real estate and their housing goals, their finances were an area of conflict for about 80% of the couples. It is important to understand your feelings about money and your future spouse to prevent disagreements in your marriage. It is also important to understand that the current financial situations of you both are because of your experiences as a child and your current thoughts.

It is vital and it would be wise for each of you to answer the following question before you get married.

What are your spending habits?

Are you a spender or a saver?

What are your views on being in control of the money?

How did your parents discuss or handle money while you were growing up?

Which parent was the primary contributor to the family finances, the mother, or the father?

Did you hear your parents argue about money frequently?

Did you grow up on government or public assistance?

Did you feel that your family was always struggling and there was never enough money to enjoy life?

Did your parents get a divorce leaving one parent struggling to support the family?

Did you feel that your parents couldn't afford to buy you the latest toy, name brand clothes, or electronics that your friends had?

Were you teased or bullied about your clothes or looks?

When you received money as a child were you taught to save it or spend it on toys, candy, etc?

Were you raised in a home where money wasn't an issue and your parents bought you whatever you wanted?

You and your partner's experiences as children have molded your current spending habits. If either of you felt deprived or witnessed your parents struggling, it may be the reason you are a workaholic. If either of you were teased or bullied as a child, it could cause you to shop until you drop and spend money you don't have to impress people that don't really care.

To create different results, you both will need to elevate your mind and change your mindset. Each of you should identify your current thoughts about money, whether it's positive or negative. Both of you should also delineate how you currently earn and handle money. Reprogram your money mindset to achieve financial clarity and abundance by creating a plan. Create a budget, write a vision together, and make it plain so that you both will be on the same financial path.

A budget is a financial model of the future. It's a picture in numbers to match where you want to go in the next three to five years.

Although some people may think that a traditional bank register is 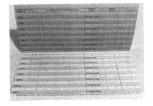 obsolete, you will need to use the register, an app, or an electronic financial program to track your finances. I have seen people lose thousands of dollars in overdraft fees because they won't balance their checking account.

You may be financially stable and someone else manages your money. That's great but you should still monitor your financial statements to avoid someone robbing you blind.

Retirement / Finances for Retirement

You want to plan for retirement and minimize your debt during your working years so that you can live comfortably. You don't want to outlive your money. Make a list of your income sources when you retire.

1. _____

2. _____

3. _____

4. _____

5. _____

6. _____

7. _____

8. _____

9. _____

10. _____

Bucket list

Where do you want to go? What are some of the things you want to accomplish? Would you both enjoy them? What will it cost and how will it affect your finances?

1. _____

2. _____

3. _____

4. _____

5. _____

6. _____

7. _____

8. _____

9. _____

10. _____

Credit Score

It's important to know how responsible your partner is with paying their bills and handling financial obligations. Credit scores range from 300-850. You need to know if your partner pays anyone. Having good credit demonstrates good money management skills. With good credit you can get lower interest rates, lower insurance premium, get funding for businesses, and leverage your credibility to build wealth.

Credit is really important in the United States. Unless you are paying cash for everything, credit is going to be a key component in your financial security. Credit is considered when purchasing a home, renting an apartment, buying a car, purchasing insurance, renting a car, getting a job, getting a promotion, and so much more.

Having bad credit is very expensive because you will always pay a higher interest rate. If you marry someone with bad credit, you may find yourself having to put everything in your name and being financially responsible for your house, cars, furniture, you name it. A person that has nothing to lose can cause you to lose everything.

Let's take a look at what a low credit score can cost you.

New Toyota Camry
$23,000
66 Month Term

Person A

Person B

Credit Score 750
Interest rate 1.99%
Payment $368.22

Credit Score 590
Interest rate 14.99%
Payment $513.97

LET'S BREAK IT DOWN!

The Formulas

Purchase Price x Interest Rate = APR
APR / 12 = Monthly Interest
Monthly Payment. - Monthly Interest =
Payment towards Principle

Monthly Interest x Months Term = Total
Interest Paid
Monthly Payment x Months Term – Total
Payments

Person A

$23,000 x 1.99% = $457.70 interest per year

$457.70 / 12 = $38.14 interest per month

$368.22 - $38.14 = $330.07 toward principle

Total Interest Paid $2,517.24
Total Payments $24,302.39

Person B

$23,000 x 14.99% = $3447.70 interest per year

$3,447.70 / 12 = $287.31 interest per month

$513.97 - $287.31 = $226.66 toward principle

$23,000 - $226.66 = $23,226.66

Total Interest Paid $18,962.46
Total Payments $33,922.02

Person B Pays
$9,619.63 MORE

Than person A for the same car and price!

If you or your partner continues to have a low credit score, you will pay more interest on your credit cards, mortgage, student loans, other loans, and more.

Rose Allure Louis, "The Credit Goddess"

Make a list of assets and liabilities so that you will have a snapshot of where you are financially.

Assets	Description	Value	Market $

Liabilities	Details	Balance	% Rate

Family

Do you want to have children? If so, how many?

Are you able to have children?

Is your partner able to have children?

Are you willing to adopt children?

Would you consider other alternatives to having children?

Starting a family or not starting a family is something that must be discussed before marriage. It is dishonest to marry someone who wants to have children knowing you are unable to have children or that you don't want to have children. That's a disaster waiting to happen. It is better to be honest upfront and make the decision together regarding what alternatives you would utilize to start a family.

When you are attracted to your partner and you find them beautiful or handsome because you love their eyes, nose, cheeks, and their lips; they all may make you want to kiss them. You imagine how your children will look with features from both of you. To avoid shock and disbelief at the birth of your child, ask your partner if they've ever had any plastic surgery. Ask for pictures of what they looked like before surgery because your children may look like the before pictures.

Family experiences mold you into who you are today. The result can be positive or negative depending on how you interpret it and apply it to your life. Watch how a man treats his mother because that's how he may treat you.

When a man wants you in his life, he will call you for no reason. Call, not text, because he wants to hear your voice. He will make every effort to spend time with you and appreciate the people who are important to you. The people who are important to him will know that you exist.

When he talks to you, he's not looking around the room, he's looking into your eyes. He listens to what you say because it matters to him. He wants to hold your hand

and show signs of affection because he's truly interested in you.

When he comes to see you, he doesn't come empty-handed, or as my godmother would say, don't allow him to come with his arms swinging. He knows the little things you like whether it's something as simple a single rose, a bouquet of flowers, or a bottle of wine. This is the behavior that most women would appreciate.

On the other hand, some ladies have daddy issues that may contribute to their abandonment issue and so much more. Perhaps her father was an amazing man and she expects her partner to fill his shoes. What she experienced during childhood could affect her expectations in the marriage.

It is wise to pay attention to what the people you love have to say about the person you're involved with. You may have heard it before, but love is blind and sometimes they see what you don't. If they are begging you to get away from your partner, then that person may not be the one for you. On the other hand, if the people you respect and trust also see what you see in your partner and encourage the relationship, that's a good sign that you two may belong together.

Family is very important to most people. I have family members who have made a major impact in my life. My grandmother, in particular, although she's not with us anymore. I miss her dearly and have come to realize that it is important to spend time with your elder relatives while they are here. It helps to have a partner that feels the same way.

Your plans for the future care of your parents is an important topic to discuss. Do either of your parents have their directives in place? If not, you need to discuss how this situation will be handled. Will either of your parents be welcome to live in your home? What about long-term care, nursing homes, and medical bills? These can add additional stress and responsibility to your marriage. What are your partner's ideas about the future care of your parents? Do you know? Do you agree? How could this change impact your relationship with your partner?

Health

Your beliefs and thoughts about health, food, and exercise could also be an issue in your relationship.

If you're a meat-lover and you marry someone who is a vegan, you could have problems at mealtime. I remember my grandmother's smothered pork chops, lima beans, rice, cornbread, and a lot of other meals she cooked. Today I don't cook or eat those foods. I rarely eat pork or red meat. When you and your partner are eating in different households, it is not as bad as it can be once you have joined households.

When you go to the doctor, you are normally asked about your family history. The doctor may ask if you know of anyone in your immediate family that has or has had cancer, diabetes, heart disease, and a list of other potential medical issues. If we continue to eat the same way our grandparents ate, we will continue to have the same illnesses that they had. As a new couple, you should make decisions on how your family will eat and maintain a healthy lifestyle.

Activity Level

If you love to work out, be active, go dancing, go on trips, and have a good time; it would be wise to marry someone with a similar activity level. If you marry someone who is a couch potato that likes to lay back and flip the remote all day it will be a struggle to get them to do anything else. This could also create tension in the relationship.

Culture differences

Diversity is apparent in today's society as there are people from different cultures and different nationalities establishing mixed relationships and having mixed children.

Potential culture differences should be considered when establishing a relationship. My mother is from Georgia and my father's family descends from the Bahamas. I love the Bahamian culture, the music, the food, and the people. I love it. I know from experience that when you are married to someone from a different culture there are a lot of differences to consider like music, movies, food, beliefs, and morals.

There were times when my ex-husband and I would watch Jamaican movies he thought were hilarious while I was looking crazy because I didn't get it. The same thing would happen when we watched some of my favorite movies or listened to some of the music I enjoyed when I was in high school. He would look at me the same way, like "ok, I don't get it."

Although all cultural differences are not bad you need to be aware that they exist and decide if you want to deal with the challenges that the differences may bring.

Blended Families and Ex-Partners

I have eight siblings and I don't share the same mother and father with any of my sisters and brothers. I love all of them. We may not see each other all the time but when we need each other, we are all there in a heartbeat. It is a wonderful thing when we all come together with our mothers and fathers and there is no drama. I know that's not the case with a lot of families. Some people love drama and confusion.

Blended families can work but the parents must set the stage and be on the same page. The parents can discuss the roles and solutions to potential issues before meeting with the children.

You should talk to the children individually and together with your spouse. It helps for the child to understand that their new stepparent is not trying to replace their biological parent. They now have both and can have a great relationship with all of them. But I will reiterate that all of the parents must be on the same page even though it can sometimes be difficult.

If the environment will not be a peaceful situation with everyone involved, then you may have to exclude some people and not extend an invitation to family functions. There must be boundaries in place for some ex's especially if they like foolishness or to create drama. Remember that exes are exes for a reason.

Past hurts and life experiences contribute to the baggage that's carried from one relationship to the next. Don't let the baggage from previous relationships weigh you down. Remember that your new partner didn't hurt you, it was the past partner. Don't let the actions of your past partners destroy what you have now.

Learn from your past mistakes so that you don't repeat them and you can make different and wiser choices that will make you a better person.

And be not conformed to this world: but be ye transformed by the renewing of your mind, that ye may prove what is that good, and acceptable, and perfect, will of God.
Romans 12:2

Mental Illness

Mental illness is real, and it is better to recognize it before you marry someone. There are more than 300 different conditions identified as mental illnesses in the Diagnostic and Statistical Manual of Mental Disorders, Fifth Edition (DSM-5)[1], which helps mental health professionals diagnose mental illnesses.

According to the healthline.com, the following are some of the most common mental illnesses affecting people in the United States:

---

[1] https://www.interiminc.org/2019/03/01/what-are-the-different-types-of-mental-illness/?gclid=Cj0KCQjwrMHsBRCIARIsAFgSeI05_j_5GUlZDMuaJDPBdAsBvTAWV8E1fR-BVDZ_0XzSAuRtdU2SeIaAl42EALw_wcB

Bipolar disorder

Bipolar disorder is a chronic mental illness that affects about 2.6 percent of Americans each year. It is characterized by episodes of energetic, manic highs and extreme, sometimes depressive lows. These can affect a person's energy level and ability to think reasonably. Mood swings caused by bipolar disorder are much more severe than the small ups and downs most people experience on a daily basis.

Persistent depressive disorder

Persistent depressive disorder is a chronic type of depression. It is also known as dysthymia. While dysthymic depression isn't intense, it can interfere with daily life. People with this condition experience symptoms for at least two years. About 1.5

percent of American adults experience dysthymia each year.

Generalized anxiety disorder

Generalized anxiety disorder (GAD) goes beyond regular everyday anxiety, like being nervous before a presentation. It causes a person to become extremely worried about many things, even when there's little or no reason to worry. Those with GAD may feel very nervous about getting through the day. They may think things won't ever work in their favor. Sometimes worrying can keep people with GAD from accomplishing everyday tasks and chores. GAD affects about 3 percent of Americans every year.

Major depressive disorder

Major depressive disorder (MDD) causes feelings of extreme sadness or hopelessness that lasts for at least two weeks. This condition is also called clinical depression. People with MDD may become so upset about their lives that they think about or try to commit suicide. About 7 percent of Americans experience at least one major depressive episode each year.

Obsessive-Compulsive Disorder

Obsessive-compulsive disorder (OCD) causes constant and repetitive thoughts, or obsessions. These thoughts happen with unnecessary and unreasonable desires to carry out certain behaviors, or compulsions. Many people with OCD realize that their thoughts and actions are unreasonable, yet they cannot stop them.

More than 2 percent of Americans are diagnosed with OCD at some point in their lifetime.

Post-Traumatic Stress Disorder (PTSD)

Post-traumatic stress disorder (PTSD) is a mental illness that's triggered after experiencing or witnessing a traumatic event. Experiences that can cause PTSD can range from extreme events, like, war, and national disasters, to verbal or physical abuse. Symptoms of PTSD may include flashbacks or being easily startled. It's estimated that 3.5 percent of American adult's experience PTSD.

Schizophrenia

Schizophrenia impairs a person's perception of reality and the world around them. It interferes with their connection to other people. It's a serious condition that needs treatment. They might experience hallucinations, have delusions, and hear voices. These can potentially put them in a dangerous situation if left untreated. It's estimated that 1 percent of the American population experiences schizophrenia.

Social anxiety disorder

Social anxiety disorder, sometimes called social phobia, causes an extreme fear of social situations. People with social anxiety may become very nervous about being around other people. They may feel like they're being judged. This can make it hard to meet new people and attend social gatherings. Approximately 15 million adults in the United States experience social anxiety each year.

Narcissist

A narcissist is someone who is unable to interact in the world in a healthy, loving way. They have no sense of self – so they must obtain a sense of self from others. This means they have no foundation for their behavior, and it leaves them open to choices that hurt others. People with narcissistic traits are dangerous. Narcissistic behaviors include:

- ✓ Lying / Secrets
- ✓ Pornography Use
- ✓ Cheating Emotionally & Physically
- ✓ Obsessing About Perceived Slights
- ✓ Anger disproportionate to the circumstance
- ✓ Property Damage – punching walls, throwing things
- ✓ Physical Intimidation – yelling and spitting in your face

Are you dating a narcissist or someone dealing with any of these mental illnesses? Look for the signs before you get married. You need to decide if this is something you want to deal with for the rest of your life. If you're already married to someone dealing with a mental illness, you may want to assist them with getting help. If they won't and your life is in danger, you may want to save yourself.

What are your must-haves and your non-negotiables?

When you are considering what you want in a relationship you need to be clear about what you want. What are your must-haves? What are your non-negotiables? What are your deal breakers? You will get what you require in a relationship so be specific about what you want. Make a list of what you require and the things you won't tolerate and keep them in front of you. Remember there are no do-overs in life so be clear about what you want.

Must Haves

1. _____

2. _____

3. _____

4. _____

5. _____

6. _____

7. _____

8. _____

9. _____

10. _____

Non-negotiables

1. _____

2. _____

3. _____

4. _____

5. _____

6. _____

7. _____

8. _____

9. _____

10. _____

The Wedding Day Promise

We are gathered here today before God, our families, and friends to celebrate the marriage of this Groom and Bride. We are gathered to rejoice in the gift of love that our Creator shares with us. We affirm today that God who is both the Creator and Sustainer of life desires us to fully experience our humanity.

We offer praise and thanks to God who has blessed us with the wonder of life, breathe, hearts, minds, and souls. We rejoice in the realization that we are most alive when we wholeheartedly embrace the gifts that God has given us, especially God's gift of love in all the ways that gift is bestowed.

Today we gather for the happiest of ceremonies – the change of status from single individuals to a married couple.

Traditionally, that change is indicated by passing the bride's hand from her family to her husband-to-be.

Today is the day that this Groom and Bride will formally and publicly make their promises to one another. Although this is indeed a high point, marriage is a journey, not a destination. Marriage is more than any one single event or promise. It is a series of decisions that have been made and will continue to be made over and over again, every day that shows each of their care and concern for the one whom they love most in the world.

Marriage is a promise that is renewed daily through a couple's actions and a responsibility taken in the spirit of faith, hope, and love, that brings comfort in times of sadness and heightens our greatest joy.

May the promises you make this day live always in your hearts and in your home so that all which you share will deepen and grow through the years, leading you through a lifetime of happiness.

A wedding is more than a celebration of the love which lives in our Bride and Groom's hearts today. It reaches into the future and proclaims their intentions for that which tomorrow shall hold. A couple who weds is joined not only by the mutual affection and love they share, but also by their hopes, dreams and by their promises of what will be...

The promises and vows they make this day shall guide them into their common future.

Bride, will you have this Man to be your husband, and will you promise your life to him, in all love and honor, in all duty and service, in all faith and tenderness, to live with him, cherish him, and obey him according to the ordinance of God, in the holy bond of marriage?

Groom, will you have this Woman to be your wife, and will you promise your life to her in all love and honor, in all duty and service, in all faith and tenderness, to live with her, cherish her, and provide for her according to the ordinance of God, in the holy bond of marriage?

Today is the public affirmation and acknowledgment of all that you are to each other. Seemingly your relationship will be as it has always been, yet there is a power in the spoken word. May that power bring you all the warmth and closeness, security, comfort, joy, and happiness that this world has to offer.

Remember that real love never fails. Love is patient, love is kind. It's not proud. It's not rude, it's not self-seeking, it's not easily angered, and it doesn't keep a record of wrongs. Love will always protect, always trust, always hope, and always persevere.

(Exchange of Rings)

Traditionally, the passage to the status of husband and wife is marked by the exchange of rings. These rings are a symbol of the unbroken circle of love. Love freely given has no beginning and no end, no giver, and no receiver for each is the giver and each is the receiver. May these rings always remind you of the vows you have taken.

Do you take this woman to be your lawfully wedded wife? Do you vow to love her and care for her for as long as you both shall live? Do you accept her, with all of her faults and strengths, and offer yourself to her with all of your own faults and strengths? Do you promise to be a faithful and loving companion and to always put

the promises you make this day above all
else?"

Now place the ring on her finger and repeat
after me.

"I take you to be my wife. I will love and
honor you, respect and cherish you all the
days of my life."

Do you take this man to be your lawfully
wedded husband? Do you vow to love him
and care for him for as long as you both
shall live? Do you accept him, with all of
his faults and strengths, and offer yourself
to him with all of your own faults and
strengths? Do you promise to be a faithful
and loving companion and to always put
the promises you make this day above all
else?

Now place the ring on his finger and repeat after me.

I take you to be my husband I will love and honor you, respect and cherish you all the days of my life.

Unity Sand Ceremony

 Today you join your separate lives together. The two separate bottles of sand symbolize your separate lives, separate families, and separate sets of friends. They represent all that you are and all that you'll ever be as an individual. They also represent your lives before today. As these two containers of sand are poured into the third container, the individual containers of sand will no longer

exist, but will be joined together as one. Just as these grains of sand can never be separated and poured again into the individual containers, so will your marriage be united as one for all of your days.

God's Cord of Three Strands

 The braiding of the three stands demonstrates how you two are joined by God in marriage. Each strand holds special meaning.

The Gold Strand represents God and His majesty it symbolizes that the Lord Jesus has been invited by the groom and bride to the position of authority in this marriage relationship.

The Purple Strand represents the groom and his life. As a new creation in Christ, the majesty of the Groom is represented in purple. As the groom loves his wife and submits himself to the Lord, the Lord, in turn, will demonstrate His great love in this marriage relationship.

The White Strand represents the bride and her life. Having been cleansed by salvation in Christ, the Bride is represented in white. As the bride honors her husband and submits herself to the Lord, the Lord, in turn, will nurture and strengthen this marriage relationship.

In braiding these three strands together, the groom and bride demonstrate that their marriage is more than a joining of two lives together. It is a unity with God as well. They have chosen to allow God to be at the center of their marriage, woven into every aspect of it.

⁹ Two are better than one; because they have a good reward for their labour.

¹⁰ For if they fall, the one will lift up his fellow: but woe to him that is alone when he falleth; for he hath not another to help him up.

¹¹ Again, if two lie together, then they have heat: but how can one be warm alone?

¹² And if one prevail against him, two shall withstand him; and a threefold cord is not quickly broken.

On this day, the bride and groom have been woven together by God as ONE in marriage!

Ecclesiastes 4:9-12

Proclamation / Blessing

You have declared before all of us that you will live together in marriage. You have made special promises to each other, which have been symbolized by the joining of hands, taking of vows, the giving and receiving of two rings, unity sand and God knot – Cord of Three Strands. By the authority vested in me, I now pronounce you to be husband and wife, a new family, and life's partners in the name of God. Those, whom God has joined together, let no one put asunder. May the love of God surround you; the Holy Spirit keep you that you may live in faith, abound in hope, and grow in love, both now and forevermore.

You may now kiss the bride!

So many look forward to this day but, marriage is so much more than a ring, a wedding day, or a title. Marriage is a place for kindness, respect, intimacy, loyalty, and the achievement of personal integrity like no other.

Creating Peace at Home

Although you are committed to each other, your partner is not responsible for meeting your every need. Some things you will have to take care of yourself. You're married. You live together, sleep together, and maybe even work together; that is a lot of together. You don't want to suffocate each other.

Give each other space if you need a few minutes to unwind and transition from work to home. Even the closest couples need time apart. It may be a few minutes or a couple of hours, figure that out together and allow time for you both to recharge.

Someone close to me shared this list of scriptures to review as you are considering what you are willing to do to have a great relationship and peace at home. Review the list and then write your own list with scriptures to reflect on along your relationship journey.

1. Growing in the Lord

But seek ye first the kingdom of God, and his righteousness; and all these things shall be added unto you.

Matthew 6:33

2. Working as a team

And God blessed them, and God said unto them, Be fruitful, and multiply, and replenish the earth, and subdue it: and have dominion over the fish of the sea, and over the

fowl of the air, and over every living
thing that moveth upon the earth.
Genesis 1:28

[22] Wives, submit yourselves unto
your own husbands, as unto the
Lord. [23] For the husband is the head
of the wife, even as Christ is the
head of the church: and he is the
saviour of the body.
[24] Therefore as the church is subject
unto Christ, so let the wives be to
their own husbands in everything.
Ephesians 5:22-24

3. Learning to Communicate

A word fitly spoken is like apples of
gold in pictures of silver.
Proverb 25:11

A soft answer turneth away wrath:
but grievous words stir up anger.
Proverb 15:1

By long forbearing is a prince
persuaded, and a soft tongue
breaketh the bone., Proverbs 25:15
The wise in heart shall be called
prudent: and the sweetness of the
lips increaseth learning.
Proverbs 16:21

Pleasant words are as a
honeycomb, sweet to the soul, and
health to the bones.
Proverbs 16:24

4. Enjoying Intimacy

Therefore shall a man leave his
father and his mother, and shall

cleave unto his wife: and they shall

be one flesh.

Geneses 2:24

5. Managing your money

[8] Will a man rob God? Yet ye have

robbed me. But ye say, Wherein

have we robbed thee? In tithes and

offerings. [9] Ye are cursed with a

curse: for ye have robbed me, even

this whole nation. [10] Bring ye all the

tithes into the storehouse, that there

may be meat in mine house, and

prove me now herewith, saith

the LORD of hosts, if I will not open

you the windows of heaven, and

pour you out a blessing, that there

shall not be room enough to receive

it.

Malachi 3:8-10

6. Keeping up your home

Every wise woman buildeth her house: but the foolish plucketh it down with her hands.

Proverbs 14:1

7. Raising your children

Therefore Sarah laughed within herself, saying, After I am waxed old shall I have pleasure, my lord being old also?

Genesis 18:12

6 And these words, which I command thee this day, shall be in thine heart:
7 And thou shalt teach them diligently unto thy children, and shalt talk of them when thou sittest in thine house, and when thou

walkest by the way, and when thou

liest down, and when thou risest up.

Deuteronomy 6:6-7

8. Extending love to Family

[16] And Ruth said, Intreat me not to

leave thee, or to return from

following after thee: for whither

thou goest, I will go; and where

thou lodgest, I will lodge: thy

people shall be my people, and thy

God my God:

[17] Where thou diest, will I die, and

there will I be buried: the LORD do

so to me, and more also, if ought but

death part thee and me.

Ruth 1:16-17

9. Tending to your Career

37 Jesus said unto him, Thou shalt love the Lord thy God with all thy heart, and with all thy soul, and with all thy mind.
38 This is the first and great commandment.
Matthew 22:37-38

10. Making Time for Fun

13 A merry heart maketh a cheerful countenance: but by sorrow of the heart the spirit is broken.
Proverbs 15:13

11. Serving the Lord

30 I can of mine own self do nothing: as I hear, I judge: and my judgment is just; because I seek not mine own will, but the will of the Father which hath sent me.

John 5:30

[28] Even as the Son of man came not to be ministered unto, but to minister, and to give his life a ransom for many.

Matthew 20:28

[21] For even hereunto were ye called: because Christ also suffered for us, leaving us an example, that ye should follow his steps:

1 Peter 2:21

[13] For, brethren, ye have been called unto liberty; only use not liberty for an occasion to the flesh, but by love serve one another.

Galatians 5:13

1. _____

2. _____

3. _____

4. _____

5. _____

6. _____

7. _____

8. _____

9. _____

10. _____

11. _____

12. _____

13. _____

14. _____

15. _____

16. _____

17. _____

18. _____

19. _____

20. _____

The Man I Desire

First and foremost I desire a man that has a real relationship with God. I desire a man who is striving for excellence in every aspect of life. I love talking to a man who is intellectually stimulating.

I desire a man who is striving for mental excellence because I need good conversation and mental stimulation. I'm not attracted to a simple-minded man.

I desire a man who is striving for spiritual excellence because I don't need to be unequally yoked... believers mixed with unbelievers is a recipe for disaster.

I desire a man who is striving for financial excellence because I don't need a financial burden.

I desire a man who is sensitive enough to understand what I go through as a woman, but strong enough to keep me grounded.

I desire a man who has integrity in relationships. A strong man doesn't have time to play games.

I desire a man who is family-oriented. One who can be the leader, provider, and the man that God has called him to be.

I desire a man I can respect. In order to be submissive, I must respect him. I cannot be submissive to a man who isn't taking care of his business.

I desire a man who knows what he wants so that when he finds me, he will recognize himself in me. God made woman to be a help-mate for man. I can't help a man if he can't help himself.

I desire a man who will recognize that I am worth this and more.

Final Thoughts

Delight thyself in the Lord and he
shall give thee the desires of thine
heart.

Psalm 37:4

Oh, taste and see that Lord is good;
Blessed is the man who trust is Him!

Psalm 34:8

God wants us to be happy and to live in good health. He wants us to have financial independence and lack for nothing. God wants us to have a great marriage with peace in our homes; if that's the desire of our hearts. We may choose to be single and that's ok.

Cast all your cares upon the Lord. Spend time delighting yourself in the Lord and He will leave your heart and mind in perfect peace. God loves us and wants the best for us. He wants to bless us beyond our wildest imagination. All God wants in return is that we do things His way. When we do things our way, we will reap what we've sown.

Life was meant to be lived. God gave us life so we should bless Him and show Him that we love and appreciate it. Someone very special to me said, "Life is God's gift to us and what we do with our life is our gift to God.

Quick Scripture References

1 Corinthians 7:3

Let the husband render unto the wife due benevolence: and likewise, also the wife unto the husband.

1 Corinthians 7:4-5

4 The wife hath not power of her own body, but the husband: and likewise, also the husband hath not power of his own body, but the wife.

5 Defraud ye not one the other, except it be with consent for a time, that ye may give yourselves to fasting and prayer; and come together again, that Satan tempt you not for your incontinency.

1 Corinthians 11:3

But I would have you know that the head of every man is Christ: and the head of the woman is the man: and the head of Christ is God.

1 Corinthians 13:4-8

[4] Charity suffereth long, and is kind; charity envieth not; charity vaunteth not itself, is not puffed up,

[5] Doth not behave itself unseemly, seeketh not her own, is not easily provoked, thinketh no evil;

[6] Rejoiceth not in iniquity, but rejoiceth in the truth;

[7] Beareth all things, believeth all things, hopeth all things, endureth all things.

[8] Charity never faileth: but whether there be prophecies, they shall fail; whether there be tongues, they shall cease; whether there be knowledge, it shall vanish away.

2 Corinthians 6:14

Be ye not unequally yoked together with unbelievers: for what fellowship hath righteousness with unrighteousness? and what communion hath light with darkness?

Deuteronomy 6:6-7

6 And these words, which I command thee this day, shall be in thine heart:
7 And thou shalt teach them diligently unto thy children, and shalt talk of them when thou sittest in thine house, and when thou walkest by the way, and when thou liest down, and when thou risest up.

Ecclesiastes 4:9-12

9 Two are better than one; because they have a good reward for their labour.

10 For if they fall, the one will lift up his fellow: but woe to him that is alone when he falleth; for he hath not another to help him up.

11 Again, if two lie together, then they have heat: but how can one be warm alone?

[12] And if one prevail against him, two shall withstand him; and a threefold cord is not quickly broken.

Ephesians 5:22-24

[22] Wives submit yourselves unto your own husbands, as unto the Lord.

[23] For the husband is the head of the wife, even as Christ is the head of the church: and he is the saviour of the body.

[24] Therefore as the church is subject unto Christ, so let the wives be to their own husbands in everything.

Galatians 5:13

[13] For, brethren, ye have been called unto liberty; only use not liberty for an occasion to the flesh, but by love serve one another.

Genesis 1:28

And God blessed them, and God said unto them, Be fruitful, and multiply, and replenish the earth, and subdue it:

and have dominion over the fish of the sea, and over the fowl of the air, and over every living thing that moveth upon the earth.

Genesis 18:12

Therefore, Sarah laughed within herself, saying, After I am waxed old shall I have pleasure, my lord being old also?

Genesis 2:24

Therefore, shall a man leave his father and his mother, and shall cleave unto his wife: and they shall be one flesh.

James 1:8

A double minded man is unstable in all his ways.

John 5:30

[30] I can of mine own self do nothing: as I hear, I judge: and my judgment is just; because I seek not mine own will, but

the will of the Father which hath sent
me.

Malachi 3:8-10

[8] Will a man rob God? Yet ye have
robbed me. But ye say, Wherein have
we robbed thee? In tithes and offerings.

[9] Ye are cursed with a curse: for ye
have robbed me, even this whole
nation.

[10] Bring ye all the tithes into the
storehouse, that there may be meat in
mine house, and prove me now
herewith, saith the LORD of hosts, if I
will not open you the windows of
heaven, and pour you out a blessing,
that there shall not be room enough to
receive it.

Matthew 6:33

[33] But seek ye first the kingdom of God,
and his righteousness; and all these
things shall be added unto you.

Matthew 19:6

6 Wherefore they are no more twain, but one flesh. What therefore God hath joined together, let not man put asunder.

Matthew 20:28

28 Even as the Son of man came not to be ministered unto, but to minister, and to give his life a ransom for many.

Matthew 22:37-38

37 Jesus said unto him, Thou shalt love the Lord thy God with all thy heart, and with all thy soul, and with all thy mind. 38 This is the first and great commandment.

1 Peter 2:21

21 For even hereunto were ye called: because Christ also suffered for us, leaving us an example, that ye should follow his steps:

1 Peter 3:1

Likewise, ye wives, be in subjection to your own husbands; that, if any obey not the word, they also may without the word be won by the conversation of the wives;

1 Peter 3:7

Likewise, ye husbands, dwell with them according to knowledge, giving honour unto the wife, as unto the weaker vessel, and as being heirs together of the grace of life; that your prayers be not hindered.

Proverbs 1:7

The fear of the LORD is the beginning of knowledge: but fools despise wisdom and instruction.

Proverbs 4:23

Keep thy heart with all diligence; for out of it are the issues of life.

Proverbs 7:6-15

[6] For at the window of my house I looked through my casement,

[7] And beheld among the simple ones, I discerned among the youths, a young man void of understanding,

[8] Passing through the street near her corner; and he went the way to her house,

[9] In the twilight, in the evening, in the black and dark night:

[10] And, behold, there met him a woman with the attire of an harlot, and subtil of heart.

[11] (She is loud and stubborn; her feet abide not in her house:

[12] Now is she without, now in the streets, and lieth in wait at every corner.)

[13] So she caught him, and kissed him, and with an impudent face said unto him,

¹⁴ I have peace offerings with me; this day have I payed my vows.

¹⁵ Therefore came I forth to meet thee, diligently to seek thy face, and I

Proverbs 7:18-19

¹⁸ Come, let us take our fill of love until the morning: let us solace ourselves with loves.

¹⁹ For the goodman is not at home, he is gone a long journey:

Proverbs 7:21-27

²¹ With her much fair speech she caused him to yield, with the flattering of her lips she forced him.

²² He goeth after her straightway, as an ox goeth to the slaughter, or as a fool to the correction of the stocks;

²³ Till a dart strike through his liver; as a bird hasteth to the snare, and knoweth not that it is for his life.

²⁴ Hearken unto me now therefore, O ye children, and attend to the words of my mouth.

²⁵ Let not thine heart decline to her ways, go not astray in her paths.

²⁶ For she hath cast down many wounded: yea, many strong men have been slain by her.

²⁷ Her house is the way to hell, going down to the
chambers of death.

Proverbs 14:1

14 Every wise woman buildeth her house: but the foolish plucketh it down with her hands.

Proverbs 15:1-2

1 A soft answer turneth away wrath: but grievous words stir up anger.

² The tongue of the wise useth knowledge aright: but the mouth of fools poureth out foolishness.

Proverbs 15:13

[13] A merry heart maketh a cheerful countenance: but by sorrow of the heart the spirit is broken.

Proverbs 16:21

[21] The wise in heart shall be called prudent: and the sweetness of the lips increaseth learning.

Proverbs 16:24

[24] Pleasant words are as an honeycomb, sweet to the soul, and health to the bones.

Proverbs 18:22

Whoso findeth a wife findeth a good thing, and obtaineth favour of the LORD.

Proverb 25:11

[11] A word fitly spoken is like apples of gold in pictures of silver.

Proverbs 25:15

[15] By long forbearing is a prince persuaded, and a soft tongue breaketh the bone.

Romans 12:2

And be not conformed to this world: but be ye transformed by the renewing of your mind, that ye may prove what is that good, and acceptable, and perfect, will of God.

Ruth 1:16-17

[16] And Ruth said, Intreat me not to leave thee, or to return from following after thee: for whither thou goest, I will go; and where thou lodgest, I will lodge: thy people shall be my people, and thy God my God:

[17] Where thou diest, will I die, and there will I be buried: the LORD do so to me, and more also, if ought but death part thee and me.

Dr. Carlisa M. Smith

To read more from Dr. Carlisa M. Smith, visit
DrCarlisa.com

Women Inspiring Nations

Speaking My Truth

Entrepreneur Elevation

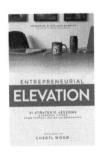

About the Author

Dr. Carlisa M. Smith  is an international speaker, bestselling author, real estate empire builder, and life coach. Dr. Carlisa is a highly sought-after speaker, known to Educate, Inspire and Empower. Dr. Carlisa ignites her audience with her enthusiastic personality, captivating smile, and intoxicating humor.

Dr. Carlisa's empowerment platform is executed through multi-media, live and virtual platforms that provide training in the areas of wealth building, life skills, personal growth, and leadership.

Education:

Doctor of Education EdD

Concentration: Organizational Leadership, Adult Education

Master of Business Administration (MBA)

Specialization – Human Resource Management

Bachelor of Business Administration

Bachelor of Ministry

Licensed Real Estate Broker & Instructor

Graduate Realtor Institute (GRI)

Seller Representative Specialist (SRS)

Senior Real Estate Specialist (SRES)

Certified Distress Property Expert (CDPE)

REO Certified Designation

Professional Affiliations:

National Coalition of 100 Black Women (NCBW)

National Associations of Realtors

National Association of Professional Women

Florida Realtors: Board of Director, Business Trends and Technology Forum, Professional Standard Forum

Realtor Association of the Palm Beaches: Board of Directors, Professional Development Committee Chair, Committee Member, Grievance Committee Member, Realtor Image Committee Chair

As an entrepreneur, Dr. Carlisa is CEO of multiple organizations including J. Briann Realty Group, Inc. She has over 26 years of experience and is known for her work ethic, commitment to excellence, integrity, persistent attention to detail, and accuracy. She is also known as an established leader and educator committed to helping others succeed and build their empire.

As a philanthropist, Dr. Smith is the founder and CEO of A Smile For Everyone, Inc. a nonprofit organization that strives to remove barriers that prevent participants from being able to pay the out of pocket expenses to maintain a healthy smile. The A Smile for Everyone team is constantly working to discover new ways to break through barriers so all of their participants can achieve the smile they deserve and desire! Allow A Smile For Everyone, Inc. to assist you with the cost to Keep Your Smile or Get Your Smile Back.

Dr. Carlisa is a Florida native and currently resides in West Palm Beach, Florida. In her spare time, she likes to travel, listen to live music, and sing.

If you are interested in booking Dr. Carlisa for your next event or want information about her programs, please contact us via Email: info@drcarlisa.com
Phone: 561-688-1316

Made in the USA
Columbia, SC
22 March 2023

14133023R00074